My Mommy is a Blogger!

written by Sommer Poquette

published by Green and Clean Mom Press

All Inquiries Should Be Addressed To:
Green and Clean Mom Press
www.greenandcleanmom.org

First Edition: June 2011
Library of Congress Control Number: 2011927628
ISBN: 978-0-615-47870-8

This book has met publication standards established by
Book Bridge Press, earning it the Book Bridge Press Seal of Excellence.
www.bookbridgepress.com

Printed on recycled paper.

CPSIA Facility Code: BP 312267

Thank you to my husband John and my children for their patience, love, support and encouragement, and to my friends and fellow bloggers who inspire me. I couldn't have done this without my sister Haley, thanks for always believing in me.

Sommer

It was early morning on career day.

Mrs. Howard's kindergarten room was bustling with students eager to tell about their parent's job.

But one little girl was more excited than the rest.
Her name was Josie.

"This is my mommy. She is a booger!"

The other students laughed when Josie said this, but Mrs. Howard gave them a stern look.

Josie's mom smiled.

"That's almost right, Josie. But I'm not a booger. I am a blogger."

The room fell quiet. The students did not know what a blogger was, so Josie tried to explain.

"My mom writes stuff on the computer. Her job is to jump up and down when she sees a good oogle number."

The children laughed again, and one student raised her hand to ask, "You get to play a jumping game for your job?"

"Yes, in a way," said Josie's mom. "My job is to find words to express my ideas and opinions to the world. I choose them carefully, and then write them down in a way that will be clear to others.

I share what I write by posting it on my internet page. It's called a blog. When other people like my blog, I get a high number rank on my page. It's like getting an A on a test!"

"And when she gets a good rank," added Josie, "she does a crazy happy dance!"

"So bloggers are dancers?" asked one student.

"No, bloggers aren't dancers," said Josie's mom, "but we feel happy when people like what we have written, because when they like it, they might pass it on to someone else."

Josie interrupted matter-of-factly. "It's called chirping."

One student in the back of the room couldn't help but blurt out, "You mean to tell me bloggers dance AND chirp?"

"Actually," said Josie's mom, "when that happens it's called a tweet. And then when I give my view about something and another person shares it with someone else, it's called a retweet."

"Last week my mom got retweeted 85 times!" exclaimed Josie.

"And when she's not dancing or tweeting, she's having parties in the kitchen!"

One little girl could not believe what she heard.
"You get to have parties for your job? Are there presents?
Do you get cake?" she asked.

"It's not that type of party," said Josie's mom, "but it still is fun because I connect with people all over the world who want to share their thoughts and opinions about products, services, and favorite things too.

A lot of them are mommy bloggers like me. When we connect to talk, we call it a party. We don't get cake, but sometimes there are prizes to win!"

"You get to win prizes for going to work? That sounds like more fun than any job ever!" said the little girl.

"But prizes aren't the only fun thing," added Josie.
"Everybody gets a nickname in blog world!"

Josie's mom smiled. "Well not everyone, but many do.
When you use a computer, privacy is important. Most people
use nicknames so they aren't sharing their real name with
people they don't know. It's a good habit."

"I have a nickname," added the boy with curly hair.
"It's Green Frog Super Hero!"

"Well," said Josie, "then you might know my mom from super
hero world. Her nickname is Green Mom and she's a
super hero too!"

The class gasped. "I don't believe you,"
snapped one student.

Mrs. Howard raised her eyebrow.

"She most definitely is a super hero!" answered Josie.

"She…fights…trolls!"

Josie's mom answered. "The sort of troll I battle doesn't live under a desk. Someone who writes an unkind comment on a person's blog is called a troll. This is not a nice thing to do, and nobody likes it when people use words to be cruel or unkind."

"So how do you fight them?" asked the girl with pigtails.

"I fight them by ignoring them," said Josie's mom. "It's like having secret anti-troll spray. I ignore them and they go away."

"That's how you have to treat bullies on the playground," said the girl.

Josie added, "And speaking of playgrounds, there's a sandbox in my mom's computer and she gets to go to school whenever she wants!"

Josie's mom laughed. "I don't really have a sandbox in my computer, but blogging is like a big sandbox for grown-ups because it's a place to share ideas.

It feels like I am always going to school because I go to conferences and classes where I learn how to write better, how to use the computer better, and all sorts of other new things so I can be the best at my blogging job."

"But how is it a job, really?" This time it wasn't a student, but Mrs. Howard asking the question.

"Let's say Mr. Brown the grocer wants people to buy his apples. He can send me an apple to try. If I like it, I will find the best words to describe his apples and tell the world how tasty they are.

When people read my opinion, they may share it with others, and soon more people will visit his store to buy apples!"
Mrs. Howard smiled. She understood now.

But another student raised his hand.
"Does that mean you get paid in apples?"

"Sometimes I get paid in apples," laughed Josie's mom. "But most often I get paid like everyone else, from businesses or people that I help through my blogging."

"So you dance, chirp, and write about apples. Do all bloggers write about apples?" asked another student.

"Bloggers tend to write about the things they care about most. I think it's good to recycle, and I like to find and suggest new products that are safe for families to use. I write about those things. Some moms write about dogs, cars, cooking or traveling. A blogger can write about anything!"

"And best yet," shouted Josie, "she can do it in her pajamas!"

"That's the best job ever!" shouted a boy in the front row.

"Because my computer is in my home, it means my job is in my home. If I wake up early and have a message, I might answer it in my pajamas. It's sort of like answering the telephone in your pajamas."

"I have really cool pajamas so I could be a blogger too," the boy added.

"It is fun," said Josie's mom to the class. "I get to share my stories and opinions with people to help businesses grow. The words I use help people make good decisions about what they buy. In this way, I help companies sell their products. When you grow up, what would you like to blog about?"

"Dolls! Ice cream! Bike riding!" the shouts rang throughout the classroom.

Josie was thrilled her mom came to school to talk about her job. She felt very proud.

"My mommy is a blogger. And I'm so lucky!"

Sommer Poquette is the blogger behind Green and Clean Mom and an early childhood consultant for Great Start. A busy mom of two, she can easily be coined a "digital mom" as she harnesses her passion for children and education. She started blogging in 2007 about her adventures in parenting and going green which led her to be a serial entrepreneur, turning her online property into a business. Helping brands large and small market to moms online, understand the green space, and use social media to reach their target audience is what Sommer craves to do in her spare time – after she's written a children's book, cooked dinner, fed the dog and brushed her teeth!

Her experiences range from social media and marketing consulting, brand ambassador and spokesperson roles, custom online campaigns, private hourly consultation for small women business owners, product reviews, and more. You can learn more about Sommer at:
Green and Clean Mom <http://greenandcleanmom.org/> and
Great Start <http://greatstartforkids.com/>.